YOUR GUIDE TO
South Carolina
Personal Injury &
Workers' Compensation

YOUR GUIDE TO
South Carolina
Personal Injury &
Workers' Compensation

This publication is intended to educate the general public about personal injury, civil litigation, and workers' compensation issues. The information contained in this publication is not legal advice. Nor does your receipt or purchase of this book in any way create an attorney-client relationship with me.

This book is in no way a description or characterization of the quality of my firm's representation. Nor should it be taken as a guarantee of a specific result in any case you may have. Every case is different.

Designed and published by

Word Association Publishers
205 Fifth Avenue
Tarentum, Pennsylvania 15084

www.wordassociation.com
1.800.827.7903

For my dad, who taught me the value of hard work.

[TABLE OF CONTENTS]

[FOREWORD]

As a lawyer, my responsibilities extend far beyond the courtroom. For I am not only an advocate, but a resource in our community. I possess the unique opportunity to provide my fellow South Carolinians with a great deal of information concerning their legal rights and responsibilities. It is why I wrote this book, and why its pages are filled with straightforward answers and safety tips rather than confusing legalese.

Safety rules are violated everyday, people get hurt, and there will always be work for attorneys. However, I believe it is my duty not only to protect the rights of injured people, but to help create a safer community. As a lawyer, I must work to strengthen the city, state, and nation in which I live. Our good name can only be restored with good acts.

Many people have helped me along my chosen path. They are too numerous to count, and there are not enough pages to thank them all. If you are one of them, know that you have my undying gratitude even if your name does not appear in this book. With that said, I must give special recognition to my family for always loving and believing in me; to Jason Savage for teaching me friendship and empathy; to Brooke McAbee and Will Payne for sharing my vision of this practice, then sacrificing to achieve it; to Neal Lourie, Tish Alleyne, and everyone at the Lourie Law Firm for showing me what it means to be a lawyer; to Gracie Faulkenberry for allowing me to share my heart; and to all my clients – for without you none of this would be possible.

CHAPTER 1

Personal Injury Law

SC PERSONAL INJURY LAW: WHAT IT MEANS AND WHY IT MATTERS

When people ask what areas of law I focus on, I usually say something like "personal injury and workers' compensation." I often follow-up with a short pitch on what personal injury and workers' compensation really mean. I've found that most people share the misconceptions I had about these areas of law before I began to practice. SC personal injury law is far more complex than a television ad or slogan attempts to portray. Likewise, only a small percentage of South Carolina's personal injury lawyers advertise through mass media.

Our state's personal injury laws are designed to place an injured party back in the position he/she enjoyed prior to being harmed by a negligent, careless, or reckless party. SC personal injury claims and lawsuits may be filed against individuals or businesses, as the law is intended to hold all at-fault parties responsible for an injury. An injured person may recover damages (i.e. money) for medical expenses, lost wages, mental anguish, lost enjoyment of life, future expenses, and a number of other well-recognized losses. In sum, SC personal injury law may be understood as the rights and responsibilities of injured people, as well as those that caused the harm. Auto accidents, unsafe products, medical malpractice, nursing home negligence, property hazards, animal attacks, and wrongful death, are but a few examples of the countless ways a personal injury case may arise.

3 THINGS YOU SHOULD KNOW ABOUT SC PERSONAL INJURY LAW

First, personal injury law is not limited to one type of client or claim. Insurance companies have spent millions and millions of dollars stereotyping injured people and the attorneys who represent them. I believe certain advertisements have severely damaged my profession's reputation. Dishonest people feigning phantom injuries have biased juror attitudes toward the truly injured. Despite these facts, one great truth remains: every day accidents occur, tragedies strike our communities, and families are left asking questions. Tragedy has no regard for race, ethnicity, neighborhood, or professional standing. Many people ask "Why do bad things happen to good people?" This is a question for which we have no answer, but we can promise that when such things happen, we are here for the people who need us.

Second, every personal injury case is different. Many factors affect a case's value, including: medical expenses, lost wages, lost earning capacity, permanent injury, the need for future medical care, the jurisdiction in which the injury occurred, and witness statements. However, two factors more than any others influence the value of a personal injury case: the defendant's conduct and our client's character. On the one hand, liability drives damages. On the other, credibility is a client's greatest asset.

Third, if you have health insurance, you should submit it to all medical providers for treatment related to your accident. In truth, being insured is a major advantage for injured people. Health insurance allows you to get treatment where you might otherwise not be able to afford it. If you're in an accident, one of the items we will demand the at-fault party's insurance company to pay for is your medical expenses. The term "medical expenses" is not defined by what you pay, but rather the true cost or value of the treatment you receive. For example, if your health insurance co-pays total $300, but the pre-adjustment cost of your medical care is $10,000, our demand would be based in part on $10,000 in medical expenses. To allow an at-fault party to offset its liability based on what your health insurance company pays would undo the notion of liability altogether, and is therefore prohibited.

HOW DO MY MEDICAL BILLS GET PAID AFTER AN ACCIDENT?

Nearly all of my personal injury clients have questions related to the payment of medical bills. Many people have been led to believe that the at-fault party's insurance company will immediately begin paying for medical care after the accident. This is a myth that SC accident lawyers must dispel. In order to help the public better understand the process by which medical bills are paid after an injury is sustained, I created the following summaries.

FOR SOUTH CAROLINIANS WITH HEALTH INSURANCE

If you have health insurance, you should use it for all treatment related to your accident. In other words, present your health insurance card and request that all medical providers submit their bills to your health insurance company. Whether you pay your insurance co-pay is up to you. My firm cannot pay your outstanding balance until your case settles or a jury award is received. Moreover, the at-fault party's insurance carrier generally will not make an offer on your case until medical bills and records have been submitted. In practical terms, that means time will pass between the date of your accident and the date you may receive a settlement or jury award. For this reason and many more, we strongly encourage clients with health insurance to use it for all injuries caused by their accident.

If money damages are recovered by way of settlement or trial, those proceeds will first be used to pay back your health insurance company's lien. We work to reduce the lien to ensure our clients recover the greatest possible sum. Money damages are also intended to reimburse you for all co-pays. Further, if there are any outstanding medical bills at the time your case concludes, we will use the settlement funds/jury award to zero out all balances. Put differently, we write checks directly to medical providers and health insurance companies as a service to our clients when their case comes to an end. My clients are therefore left with no outstanding medical bills or liens at the conclusion of most cases.

FOR SOUTH CAROLINIANS WITHOUT HEALTH INSURANCE

If you DO NOT have health insurance, your SC injury attorney cannot pay for your medical treatment without violating his/her ethical obligations. A common misconception is that attorneys are responsible for selecting and paying their clients' doctors. This practice is not employed by my firm. Rather, I seek qualified doctors willing to treat uninsured patients based on "letters of protection." These letters are sent by me, to your treating physician or therapist, and serve to protect the doctor's fee with a legal promise that the medical professional will be paid out of your settlement/jury award proceeds. Not all doctors accept letters of protection.

If damages are recovered by way of settlement or trial, those proceeds will first be used to pay back your medical bills. In some instances, hospitals and other care providers will reduce your medical bill to assist us in reaching a fair settlement. If there are any outstanding medical bills at the time your case concludes, we will use the settlement funds/jury award to zero out all balances. Put differently, we write checks directly to medical providers as a service to our clients when their case comes to an end. Clients are therefore left with no outstanding medical bills at the conclusion of most cases.

LOST WAGES: THE MONEY YOU LOST MAY BE RECOVERED IN A SC PERSONAL INJURY CLAIM

SC personal injury clients may recover lost wages caused by another's wrongdoing so long as a few elements are met. First, we must prove that another person or business is in fact at-fault for your injury. We have to establish liability. Second, we must prove that your injury prevented you from working. This second element often requires medical evidence in the form of a work-excuse. If a doctor does not give you a work-excuse, it is hard to recover lost wages. Insurance companies will try to argue that you could have worked after your accident if a doctor does not state otherwise. I am currently fighting this battle in multiple cases.

I tell every injured client the same thing: "If you can work, you should. If you can't work because of your injuries, you need to tell your doctor exactly what your job requires and ask whether you can return to work. You then need to contact your employer and provide him/her with any work-excuse."

Many doctors place injured workers on light duty. If you are placed on light duty, you should inform your employer of this fact, and attempt to perform any light duties available at your job. If there is no light duty available, you can either stay out-of-work, attempt to perform regular duties at your own risk, or seek a light duty job. No matter which option a client chooses, if he/she loses any income because of a personal injury, we will seek to recover all lost earnings. Furthermore, even if you receive a paycheck during your time out-of-work based on disability coverage or paid-time-off, you may still recover lost wages for any time missed. The at-fault party is not allowed to pay you less simply because you have disability insurance or vacation days.

Put simply, every dollar you lose because of your accident may be regained so long as the law and medical evidence is on our side.

THE TRUTH BEHIND FREE CONSULTATIONS

Nearly all Columbia, SC injury lawyers offer free consultations. You have probably seen the ads in the yellow pages and on television. Even my website mentions free consultations for the truly injured. In other words, the promise of a free consultation should not determine which personal injury lawyer you choose. Moreover, there are a number of questions you should ask before taking time out of your day to travel to a "free" consultation.

First, ask the person you speak with on the phone whether your free consultation will be with an attorney, paralegal, or intake coordinator. At my firm, I personally handle all initial consults, as I believe it critical to establish a relationship of trust and honesty with clients from the outset.

Second, ask what percentage of the attorney's practice is devoted to personal injury. This information is often available on the lawyer's website if you cannot get an answer over the phone.

Third, ask whether the attorney has handled similar cases in the past. Within the world of personal injury, some lawyers focus on specific subfields such as medical malpractice or products liability. If you have a complex case, you will want to know whether the attorney you are contacting has achieved a positive result in a case that resembles yours.

Fourth, ask the injury lawyer about her fees. Almost every personal injury case is handled on a contingency basis. In other words, you do not have to pay the lawyer a fee unless she recovers money for you. Injury attorneys rarely charge a retainer fee or hourly rate in an injury case. That is why consultations are free. Additionally, not all contingency fees equal 33%. Some attorneys charge 40% or more for personal injury cases.

Prior to meeting with me, I encourage potential clients to visit my website, read our free literature, and learn as much as possible about the firm. As your time is not free, I do my best not to take it without knowing first determining whether your case has merit. This is why I engage in phone conversations regarding a potential client's case before she ever comes in for a free consultation with me.

QUESTIONS YOU SHOULD ASK BEFORE HIRING AN ATTORNEY

1. **How can you help me?**

I will first assess whether you need a lawyer. Not every legal problem requires an attorney, and it may be in your best interest to proceed without representation. However, if I believe your interests would be furthered by an attorney, I will provide a free consultation as well as free literature addressing your legal issue.

If you decide to hire my firm, we will immediately begin protecting your rights against insurance companies and all potential defendants. My firm will then guide you through the legal process and advocate on your behalf. We will collect medical records, take photographs and video if necessary, draft demand letters, and pursue your case through trial, should a fair settlement not be reached.

2. **Do you have experience with this type of case?**

Since my first week as a practicing attorney, I have been representing injured people in civil and workers' compensation matters. 100% of my practice is devoted to litigation, with a focus on personal injury and workers' compensation. More specifically, I seek to represent individuals and families in cases involving auto and trucking accidents, work-related injuries, unsafe products, nursing home negligence, property hazards, insurance disputes, consumer abuses, wrongful death and other areas of civil law.

3. What resources will you devote to my case?

My law firm is committed to maximizing the value of your case. While we attempt to reach fair settlements without need of litigation, when forced to file suit, I am willing to aggressively pursue cases through trial. I utilize a team approach to each case. You will not only have an experienced attorney working on your behalf, but also a paralegal. I further believe in presenting evidence beyond written and oral arguments. I am therefore willing to advance the costs for medical and safety experts, lifecare planners, private investigators, technology consultants, and a host of other professionals when effective advocacy requires these individuals.

4. If I come in for a free consultation, will I meet with an attorney?

At my firm, I provide all initial consultations at no cost. The firm utilizes a team approach, with each client being assigned an individual paralegal, but we believe consultations require the legal knowledge of a trained attorney. It is the attorney who develops theories of liability, applies law to fact, and takes responsibility for maximizing the value of your case. The earlier this process begins, the better it is for the client. In-person consultations also reinforce my firm's commitment to personal service.

PAST ACCIDENTS WON'T KILL YOUR CASE IF YOUR ATTORNEY KNOWS BEFORE THE INSURANCE COMPANY

I meet many clients who fear that a past accident or pre-existing condition will prevent them from recovering damages. Some injured people do not tell their attorney about the past accident out of concern that the attorney may drop the case once he/she finds out. Other injured people mistakenly believe that no one will ever uncover the past accident, so there is no reason to tell their attorney. Please, never become one of those people.

You must tell your injury lawyer all the details and effects of your past accident if you expect high quality representation. My client intake forms have a section on pre-existing conditions and old accidents. Every consultation I provide includes a discussion of any and all past accidents. As I tell my injured clients, "the insurance company will uncover every claim you have ever made, every injury you have ever sustained, so you better tell me now before it comes out in a deposition or at trial." Insurance companies spend huge amounts of money on research programs to find out whether you are a "litigious" person. Put differently, they want to know, as do I, whether you have filed injury claims in the past. So long as I know the facts of old accidents, including: what injuries you sustained, what medical treatment you received, and the last time you experienced any symptoms related to the accident, I will be able to properly assess the effects of the old injury on your case.

Unless the new accident resulted in no new medical bills, loss wages, or injury, you may still have a valid claim. The insurance company will undoubtedly argue that your problems are tied to the old injury, but medical evidence often proves otherwise. For example, if you underwent back surgery in 2005 because of a car accident, but have received no treatment and experienced little pain since 2007, you will not be prevented from bringing a new claim based on a 2012 accident that created the need for additional surgery. The law calls this causation. The idea is that you should be compensated for all medical expenses and other losses you would not have suffered "but for" another party's wrongdoing. In South Carolina, other drivers and businesses "take you as they find you." Therefore, even if you may be more vulnerable to injury, even if the same accident would not have caused such significant harm for a previously healthy person, the at-fault party must pay for every loss you experience because of the new accident.

Therefore, tell your SC accident attorney about all previous accidents and injuries. Give your attorney the tools he/she needs to fight for you. An honest, trustworthy client is often among the greatest strengths in my injury cases. Be honest with your lawyer, and trust that he/she will have the skills to maximize the strengths of your case, minimize the weaknesses, and earn you the best possible recovery.

WHAT HAPPENS AFTER AN SC PERSONAL INJURY LAWSUIT IS FILED

If the at-fault party's insurance company refuses to fairly compensate you for all your losses, we may have to file a lawsuit. I file many lawsuits every year. I wish this were not the case. It would be much easier if insurance companies simply offered fair settlements based on the harm you incurred. I would rather see clients receive money faster and with less fight, but often times a lawsuit is the only avenue to justice.

A lawsuit begins when we file a "Complaint." The Complaint contains facts about how you were injured, why the other party is at-fault, and what losses you have sustained due to their wrongdoing. The at-fault party's insurance company will hire a lawyer to defend the case after they receive the Complaint. Their lawyer will most likely file an "Answer" to the Complaint. The Answer usually denies all wrongdoing, and sometimes blames you for the accident.

The next phase of litigation is known as "discovery." It involves exactly what the word implies. We discover what evidence they intend to use at trial, and what explanations they offer as to the cause of the accident. Discovery includes written questions known as "interrogatories," demands that all evidence be produced called "requests for production," and official court proceedings called "depositions." This last term is probably familiar to you. Depositions do not have to be scary. Preparation is the key. When I "depose" the at-fault party or one of their witnesses, I ask lots of questions about safety rules, the importance of those rules, and the reasons those rules were violated. All answers are given under oath exactly like court testimony. These answers are also recorded by a court reporter, and may later be used to cross-examine the witness.

Before one of my clients is deposed, he/she meets with me and goes over all "dos/don'ts," as well as what to expect. For example, I remind all clients that "a deposition is not the time to tell your story. That is my job." My clients' answers are therefore short and to the point. So long as they tell the truth, there is no question or answer that will ruin the case.

Once depositions have been taken, the next step in the case is usually "mediation." This is when my client and I meet with the insurance adjuster and their attorney to determine whether a fair settlement can be reached. A third attorney, known as a "mediator," listens to both sides' version of facts. We are then split in two rooms, and the mediator goes back and forth to help achieve a settlement. For instance, when mediation begins our latest demand may be $300,000.00. The most recent offer may only be $10,000.00. However, at the end of mediation, we might have settled the case for somewhere between those two figures. The mediator's job is to resolve the dispute by showing both sides how much there is to lose at trial. We may have a case that could result in a verdict for the defense. The same case might, however, result in a large verdict for my client. Because both sides have so much to lose given the uncertainty of trial and the unpredictable nature of juries, a settlement could be best. If mediation fails, we begin preparing for trial. A failed mediation does not guarantee a trial—a settlement could still be reached—but it does mean we must prepare for battle.

In sum, after most personal injury lawsuits are filed, an answer will be given, discovery will be performed, mediation may be held, and a trial could take place. As I stated, it would be far simpler for the insurance company to pay you what your case is worth at the outset, but many times justice cannot be achieved without a fight. My job as an SC injury attorney is to maximize the value of your case and earn you the best possible result no matter how great the fight.

DAMAGES AND WHY YOU'LL NEVER HEAR ME SAY "PAIN AND SUFFERING"

South Carolina personal injury attorneys often talk about *damages.* These discussions take place with clients, during negotiations with the defendant's attorney, and in front of juries. So what are damages? Very simply, they are the measure of a person's losses due to another's wrongdoing. Damages are far more than *pain and suffering.*

Damages include past and future medical expenses, lost wages, and diminished earning capacity. These are examples of *monetary damages.* In non-lawyer speak, medical bills and lost income are damages directly related to your bank account. That is why we call them monetary or economic damages.

South Carolinians who have been injured due to another's negligence or intentional wrongdoing, may also be allowed to recover *non-economic damages*. Though *pain and suffering* is a commonly used term for these damages, in my job as an SC injury lawyer, I never use this phrase when speaking with clients, insurance adjusters, or defense attorneys. Pain and suffering is too narrow and too shallow of an explanation for what many personal injury clients experience after their accident. It's a lazy term that juries have been taught to listen for, and if heard, to believe someone is milking the system.

Physical pain is real. Many of my clients live with it, and will be forced to bear it the rest of their lives. However, physical pain alone rarely increases a case's value without substantial medical evidence. For this reason, we seek to present doctors' testimony and medical records that establish a percentage of permanent impairment before ever mentioning physical pain. Put simply, without the medical evidence it's the client's word against decades of bias toward personal injury clients; bias that was purchased and created by the insurance industry in their attempt to discredit plaintiffs and increase profits.

Suffering means too many things to too many people to have real value in a legal case. In contrast, most jurors can relate to reliving a moment over and over in their heads. Jurors can also imagine what it must be like to have the ability to walk at 9:34 a.m. on a Saturday morning, and by 9:35, to never be able to walk again. Therefore, instead of using the word suffering, I focus on my personal injury clients' *lost enjoyment of life* as well as their *mental anguish*. Does a former factory worker suffer every time her own child has to lift her into a wheelchair? Does a nineteen year-old suffer each time he looks in the mirror and sees the facial scars left by a drunk driver? Of course they do, but to most effectively represent such victims, we ask that damages be awarded for lost enjoyment of life, mental anguish, permanent impairment, *non-economic damages* other than pain and suffering.

All of the damages I've discussed thus far are collectively referred to as *actual damages*. They are the actual losses that a client sustained. In cases where the defendant's actions are reckless, willful or wanton (*exp. drunk driving, nursing home abuse, sexual exploitation*) punitive damages may be awarded. Despite what you hear in the media, punitive damages are rare. They are designed to punish bad behavior and to prevent it in the future. Punitive damages also lend invaluable protection to consumers. Without punitive damages, or in states where a cap on punitive damages exists, large corporations may simply calculate how much they stand to lose if sued, weigh it against the cost of making a product safe for consumers, then pick the cheaper alternative. You can thank the South Carolina legislature for passing a 2011 law that caps punitive damages.

HOW LONG WILL MY SC PERSONAL INJURY CASE TAKE?

The short answer is: "It depends." I'm frequently asked this question, but the answer never really changes. Many factors could affect the length of a personal injury case, including: a client's injuries, medical treatment, insurance coverage, liability disputes, Medicaid, Medicare, liens, and the court docket. If liability (i.e. who was at fault) is not in dispute, a case might get resolved quickly. Then again, even where liability is admitted, there may be an argument over how much money the at-fault party's insurance company owes my client. In these instances, a lawsuit might need to be filed. Once a lawsuit is filed, it is generally months and in some cases years before a dispute is resolved.

When you sustain a personal injury in South Carolina because of someone else's negligence or recklessness, you may be entitled to damages (i.e. money) for medical expenses and other losses. When I submit a demand package to the at-fault party's insurer, I therefore include your medical records in addition to relevant photos and video. However, if I am to get you compensated for all your medical expenses, I should not make a demand until one of two things happens. First, you complete all medical treatment related to the accident. Second, I get an estimate from a doctor regarding what future medical treatment you may need because of your accident. Most personal injury cases fall in the first of these two categories.

When you finish treating we request updated medical records from your last treating physician, specialist, physical therapist, etc....These records often take about one month to arrive. We then take these records, along with the rest of the demand package, and send it the at-fault party's insurance company because they are the ones writing the check. In most instances, the insurer will respond to our demand within one month. Their response begins the negotiating process. Negotiations sometimes take only days and result in a settlement. Other times they breakdown and lead to me filing a lawsuit. My goal is to reach a fair settlement without having to go through months or years of litigation, but where the insurance company is unwilling to adequately compensate my client for his or her losses, I don't hesitate to fight for justice.

WHICH DOCTOR SHOULD I GO SEE AND WHAT MEDICAL TREATMENT SHOULD I GET?

I receive many questions about medical treatment. Some injured people think it is best to avoid medical treatment. Other clients ask which doctor I want them to see. The fact is, I don't pick clients' medical providers or tell them what treatment to seek. I'm an attorney, not a medical professional. I therefore tell every client the same thing: "Describe for the doctor what problems you are having and seek all medical treatment that is reasonable and necessary."

Doctor shopping, malingering, unnecessary medical visits, and unreasonably high medical bills only hurt the value of a personal injury case. South Carolina's injured need to understand that they won't pocket more money by "gaming the system." The value of a personal injury case value is influenced by medical evidence. A credible doctor saying you are hurt goes much further than a lawyer arguing the same thing. My job is to put together the medical evidence, your total losses, the at-fault party's wrongdoing, and a number of other factors in order to maximize the value of a case.

The best medical evidence often comes as a result of clients seeking all treatment that is reasonable and necessary. It also comes as a result of personal injury clients being honest about the full extent of their injuries. There is no need to minimize how bad you got hurt. Accidents are often devastating and life-changing. Your doctor needs to know the severity of your injuries. However, your pain levels should never be overstated. So long as you are honest with your doctors, they will see that you are referred to the right specialists and therapists where necessary. The medical records will in turn provide evidence of your injury, and promote the best possible result in your personal injury case.

DOES EVERY SC PERSONAL INJURY CASE NEED A LAWYER? NO

It may surprise the public to find out that many Columbia, SC personal injury attorneys accept less than one out of every ten potential clients. The reasons are varied. Some potential clients lack credibility, others may have already missed the statute of limitations. However, the overwhelming majority of cases I turn down have nothing to do with a client's character or the statute of limitations. Rather, the injury and resulting losses are not great enough to warrant legal representation. That's right— some Columbia, South Carolina personal injury lawyers actually turn down money when we believe it is not in the client's best interest to hire us.

Often times, an auto accident will require a visit to urgent care or the emergency room. People want to get x-rayed, and ensure no major injury has been sustained. The doctor will usually send the accident victim home with narcotic and anti-inflammatory prescriptions to deal with the soreness and spasms that may follow. When no additional medical care is needed, the injured party should simply be grateful the accident was not worse. In my opinion, these are not cases that require an attorney. The injured person may collect his/her medical bills, or have them sent directly to the at-fault driver's insurance company, then negotiate the claim accordingly. Though I caution clients against recorded statements and the signing of any form sent by the at-fault driver's insurer, when liability is clear, medical treatment is minimal, and no permanent injury has been sustained, injured people might pocket more money without an attorney. Here's why: if you hire an SC accident attorney, he/she might charge up to 40% even for an accident such as the one I described. The attorney might also refuse to lessen his/her fee when a settlement is reached, even if that means the law firm receives more money than you after medical bills are paid.

Unless the accident attorney earns you a substantially larger settlement than you could have obtained on your own, you risk losing money.

Minor injury cases are far different than those involving serious harm, expensive medical treatment, lost wages, and permanent injury. In the latter instance, I highly recommend at least consulting an SC accident lawyer before ever speaking to the at-fault party's insurer or signing any documents the insurer sends you. While I am always honored to speak with a potential client, I will not represent an injured party unless I absolutely believe it is in his/her best legal and financial interest. I may have lost money turning down these cases, but I am certain it gives me more time to focus on representing the injured people who need me most.

HOW INSURANCE COMPANIES MAKE MONEY AND WHY IT MATTERS TO YOU

Insurance companies and the many people they employ are not evil. Even though I am a South Carolina personal injury lawyer, I have friends who work in the insurance field. However, you must understand that insurance is a business - and all of us are target customers. Auto, health, homeowners, and workers' comp insurance companies all earn profits the same way. They charge us premiums, then pay out as little as possible on claims. Like some (unethical) lawyer advertisements, insurance companies make grand promises and attempt to persuade the public into believing they are superior to the competition. For instance, you may hear that just a few minutes on the phone can result in big savings. The insurance company might also present itself as trustworthy, neighborly, even paternal. Based on their commercials, you would think that every insurance adjuster and executive wakes up in the morning thinking of how they can protect you. Please don't be deceived.

Remember, part of an insurance company's profit-model is to collect premiums. They need new customers. And like most other advertisements, the devil is always in the details. The initial rate you are offered may change. This happened to me shortly after I graduated from college. My monthly health insurance premium began to rise month after month. When I called the insurer to find out why, they said "Your rate is subject to increase. If you want to remain insured and avoid late fees, you need to pay your premium by the first of next month." As a 22 year-old, soon-to-be law student, I couldn't afford health insurance and didn't have the nerve to ask my father for help. The next year, a portion of my student loan went to pay for health insurance – albeit through a different, though equally unworthy insurance giant.

My experience is not unlike thousands, if not millions, of other Americans. I provide it as a cautionary tale. Don't be lured in by cheap initial offerings. Ask lots of questions, including: if the rate is fixed; which pre-existing conditions are excluded; and whether your current doctor is part of the insurer's network.

Once an insurance company has received your premium, it then tries to pay out minimal amounts on claims. This is part two of the insurer's profit model. I'll provide another example to illustrate. Let's say you have been with an auto insurance company for 10 years. You will have given them thousands of dollars in monthly or semi-annual payments. Then let's say you get in a car accident when another driver is texting rather than paying attention to a red light. You find out that the at-fault driver was uninsured. Your insurance claim is therefore made against your own company. In this instance, the neighborly company that happily collected your money for the last 10 years now has something to lose – its earnings. Rather than asking how you can be compensated for medical expenses, lost wages, mental anguish, and other damages, your own insurer may simply call you and say that if you sign a release they can get you a check for $5,000 by the next afternoon. No matter the fact that your claim may be worth five or ten times that amount, no matter your loyal patronage of their company – at the end of the day, an insurance company is issuing you a policy in hopes that they will profit. The only way to profit is to pay customers less money than they have collected from them.

I am familiar with the insurance companies' tricks and gimmicks. I know how little they offer unrepresented people, and how much good a SC injury lawyer may be able to accomplish. I have dedicated my entire professional career to representing South Carolina's truly injured, and can imagine no other job that would give me the satisfaction I find in giving an accident victim his or her life back. Insurance companies may not be evil, but neither is consulting a lawyer when insurers act as adversaries rather than friends.

CHAPTER 2

Auto Accidents

5 THINGS YOU SHOULD KNOW ABOUT AUTO ACCIDENTS IN SOUTH CAROLINA

1.   **If you are injured in an SC auto accident, you may be entitled to damages not only for your medical bills, but also for lost wages, lost earning capacity, future medical costs, mental anguish, and a number of other losses you've suffered due to your accident.**

In my work as an accident attorney, I remind clients that each case is different and there is no guarantee of recovery. However, in most cases where medical bills have been incurred, the injured party has suffered additional losses demanding compensation. The law is designed to place you in the position you enjoyed prior to your accident. Thus, for every loss you suffer, money damages may be sought.

2. You should only seek reasonable and necessary medical treatment after your auto accident.

Do not allow a pending claim or lawsuit to influence your healthcare decisions. I have met people who mistakenly believe that driving up medical bills (or oppositely, avoiding medical treatment) will result in a greater recovery. Rather than trying to "game the system," I encourage clients to apply a simple principle: seek reasonable and necessary treatment they can afford. Moreover, if you have any form of health insurance, present it to your provider at the time of treatment. A defendant's liability and the money he/she owes you is not reduced by the fact that your health insurance company paid for treatment prior to the resolution of your legal matter. Though your health insurance company may be able to demand reimbursement for some of its expenditures once your case is resolved, a defendant can never offset its liability based on a third party (i.e. your health insurer) paying for your treatment. In law this is known as the "collateral source rule;" it is a rule I apply forcefully on my clients' behalf.

3. Before filing a lawsuit, a claim is filed with the defendant's insurance company and a fair settlement is sought.

Money will never give you back the life you enjoyed prior to your accident. Nonetheless, my job as an SC injury lawyer is to maximize the value of your case by obtaining compensation for every loss you have suffered. This job is often accomplished by way of settlement. In other instances, I may have to defend your rights and file a lawsuit. My team understands that the faster you receive compensation for your losses, the sooner you can move forward with your life. We therefore work diligently to collect medical records, take photos, obtain affidavits and submit a demand package to the defendant's insurance company on your behalf – all in hopes of achieving a fair settlement of your claim. Should an insurance company prove unreasonable, we may be forced to engage in litigation, requiring discovery, mediation and trial.

4. Even if the defendant is uninsured, you may still seek compensation based on SC uninsured motorist laws.

The law requires that every auto insurance policy sold in South Carolina include uninsured motorist coverage. Therefore, if you are injured by an uninsured driver, you may still receive compensation from the insurance company that insures either you, a family member with whom you live, and/or the vehicle in which you were a passenger. Furthermore, in some instances we may be able to "stack" these uninsured policies or reform the uninsured policy to obtain greater compensation for you.

5. **Most if not all auto insurance companies are profit-driven corporations.**

Auto insurance companies have the goal of maximizing profits. Their allegiance is often to executives, board members, and shareholders. To accomplish their goals, insurance companies charge premiums while paying out as few claims as possible. Even when settlement offers are made, my experience is that initial offers to unrepresented persons are far less than what an insurance company is ultimately willing to pay – especially when they know a trained attorney is working on your behalf.

TALKING, TEXTING, EMAILING, FACEBOOK, AND PUNITIVE DAMAGES

The field of SC personal injury law includes auto and trucking accidents. Many of these accidents are as preventable as they are life-changing. In a high percentage of cases, the at-fault driver was distracted.

Before smartphones, people could not browse the internet, email, text, and talk with only one device. Now they can—even while they drive. If you've done it, you know it's dangerous. If you have trouble believing that it's as common as the media portrays, know that millions of emails and text messages are sent from drivers every year.

When a new SC auto accident client comes in for a consultation, one subject we discuss is whether the client saw the at-fault party prior to the collision. If so, I want to know if the at-fault driver was talking on a cell phone or looking down before he/she injured my client. I also talk to witnesses about whether they saw or suspected cell phone use.

If we cannot settle a case without filing a lawsuit, one of the first items I subpoena in most auto accident cases is the Defendant's cell phone records. My staff and I then check for incoming/outgoing calls, text messages, and Internet capability. We also review social media sites to determine whether any "posts" or "tweets" were made from the Defendant's phone near the time of the accident.

Many people view texting and driving as a reckless, willful act. When it causes injury to another, jurors often believe the Defendant's recklessness warrants punitive damages. For this reason, punitive damages are demanded in every lawsuit I file where the at-fault party was texting while driving. As an accident attorney my job is to maximize clients' recovery and help deter dangerous behavior. Seeking punitive damages is one part of this job in cases where another driver placed a "smartphone" ahead of my client's safety.

WHY TALKING TO THE INSURANCE COMPANY AFTER AN AUTO ACCIDENT MAY ONLY CAUSE MORE HARM

In my job, I'm often asked whether a person hurt in an auto accident should speak to the at-fault driver's insurance company. I also receive questions pertaining to medical authorizations and releases sent by the at-fault party's insurer. The answer to these questions is almost always "No."

The at-fault party's insurance company has an individual known as an "adjuster" who is responsible for assigning a dollar figure to your claim. The adjuster's loyalty is to his/her employer. Almost all insurance companies are profit-driven corporations. They exist to make money. Their goal is to maximize profits. They accomplish this goal by increasing premiums and paying out as little as possible on claims, including auto accident claims. Adjusters are well trained to listen closely to every statement you give, and then use such statements against you. In my experience, I've yet to see an auto accident victim benefit from speaking to the adjuster before consulting an attorney. This is not to say that every case requires a lawyer, but I do think it's important that you know your rights before speaking to anyone whose job is to keep as much money as possible out of your pocket.

Health care forms are designed to allow the at-fault driver's insurer to obtain your complete medical history. The adjuster will often distort your medical history in an attempt to reduce the value of your case. When I accept a new client, I have the client sign health authorizations to avoid any HIPAA violation. The form I provide clients is different than the insurance document in two key ways. First, I use the information I obtain for your benefit. Second, I only seek records that are relevant to your case. My staff and I then take these records, along with all photos, videos, affidavits, demand letter, and any other evidence that strengthens your case, and submit it to the at-fault driver's insurer.

If you sign the insurance company's release of liability form, your claim is forever settled. You will never have the opportunity to seek any additional money, even if you develop health problems years after the auto accident. A release—by definition—releases the at-fault driver as well as his/her insurance company, from all liability. In return, you receive what is generally a small amount of money. Insurance companies know that people will often accept less money if they can get it faster; they prey upon this unfortunate reality. Many times, I have heard of people being offered 2, 5, or $10,000 to settle a claim immediately after the auto accident, when in reality the case may be worth 10, 20, or 50 times what the insurer is offering. Don't cheat yourself by signing a release before at least discussing other options with a South Carolina attorney.

If you are unsure as to the extent of your injuries, your need for future medical care, or the value of your auto accident case, I strongly encourage you to first speak with a South Carolina accident attorney. I also invite you to review my website, find answers to additional questions you may have, and call me should I be of further assistance.

CAR INSURANCE, A DEER, AND I-26: WHY MORE COVERAGE SAVES MONEY IN THE END

South Carolina injury lawyers are not immune from auto accidents. Nor is the irony of the story I am about to tell lost on me. I was driving home from Charleston, passing through Orangeburg, in late-2011 when a deer wandered onto I-26. I didn't see the deer until my car was only yards from it. The collision was as unavoidable as it was violent. Fortunately, I suffered no personal injury. The same cannot be said for the deer or my car. Along with body and tire damage, the radiator had to be replaced. In all, the repair bill ran into the $1000s.

When I bought my auto insurance policy, I was offered comprehensive and collision coverage. It cost more at the time, but when I hit the deer my policy saved me those $1000s. My car accident was covered by the "comprehensive" section of the policy, so other than a small deductible, my insurance company paid for all repairs. Comprehensive coverage is exactly what it sounds like – it covers most incidents resulting in damage that would not otherwise be covered by a "liability" or "collision" policy. For example, if a tree branch fell through your back window, and no homeowners' or property coverage was available, your comprehensive auto insurance may cover the damages. Collision insurance can also be understood simply by its name. It covers collisions that you cause. Very simply, collision insurance pays for repairs to your car in the event you are at fault for an accident. Nonetheless, always go over the terms of your coverage with your insurance agent, read your policy, and check for exclusions.

I was lucky I didn't get hurt. My decision to buy full coverage had nothing to do with luck, however. I have seen enough auto accidents and known too many people who could have recovered far more money had they only purchased more insurance coverage. The next time you renew your policy, please consider the money you could safe and the debt (repair shop, hospital, physical therapist bills, etc…) you might avoid by spending a few dollars more per month. Comprehensive, collision, underinsured motorist, and additional uninsured motorist coverage is available to all of our state's drivers – even SC car accident attorneys. Please choose wisely and be safe.

UNDERINSURED MOTORIST COVERAGE: WHAT IT MEANS AND WHY IT MATTERS

South Carolina law requires that every time an auto insurance policy sold is sold in our state, a meaningful offer of underinsured coverage be made as well. Underinsured motorist ("UIM") coverage allows you to protect yourself, your passengers, and your family in the event of an accident with a driver who though insured, lacks sufficient liability coverage to pay for your injuries. Put simply, insurance coverage of this kind is meant to guard you against losses caused by "underinsured" drivers; it is meant to allow you to insure yourself against another's negligence. For example, if a driver with only minimum liability limits ($25k) runs a red light, crashes into another vehicle, and puts the innocent party in the hospital, the at-fault driver's insurance limits would not be great enough to cover the innocent party's medical bills, let alone lost wages, permanent impairment, and a host of non-economic damages.

These are the times when underinsured motorist coverage is critical. Without it, the injured party could face collection notices from medical providers and foreclosure notices from mortgage companies. Too many times, I have seen hard working people put out of work due to an accident, then collect only $25,000 in minimum liability money because he/she failed to purchase UIM coverage when given the opportunity.

UIM policies give every South Carolinian on the highway a chance to protect themselves and the people closest to them. Accidents are often unavoidable from the vantage point of the injured. The consequences are not, however. UIM coverage can lessen the financial impact on those injured by another driver's negligence or recklessness.

Rather than putting myself at the mercy of other motorist's liability limits, I purchased UIM coverage shortly after becoming an attorney. I hope that I never have to use it, though I feel safer knowing I'm covered. If you do not currently possess UIM coverage, you may consider contacting your insurance agent regarding rates. In many instances, UIM policies are less than $5 per month. I know of few things that could be of greater benefit yet cost so little.

WHAT HAPPENS IF AN UNINSURED DRIVER INJURES YOU IN SOUTH CAROLINA

I have learned that our state's auto accident and insurance law is intended to protect citizens against uninsured drivers. In fact, South Carolina law requires that every auto insurance policy sold in our state include uninsured motorist coverage. Therefore, if you are injured by an uninsured driver, you may still receive compensation from the insurance company that insures either you, a family member with whom you live, and/or the vehicle in which you were a passenger. Furthermore, in some instances we may be able to "stack" these uninsured policies or reform the uninsured policy to obtain greater compensation for you. Policy reformation depends on whether the auto insurance company that sold the uninsured policy made a "meaningful offer" of uninsured coverage up to the limits of the liability coverage.

While the legal explanation may be complicated, the takeaway is simple: if you are injured by an uninsured driver in an SC auto accident, you may be entitled to damages not only for your medical bills, but also for lost wages, lost earning capacity, future medical costs, mental anguish, and a number of other losses you've suffered due to your accident.

CHAPTER 3

Specific Types of Personal Injury Cases

5 THINGS YOU SHOULD KNOW ABOUT MEDICAL MALPRACTICE IN SOUTH CAROLINA

1.   To recover damages for medical malpractice, we must prove that a medical provider breached the standard of care, causing your injury

In South Carolina, it is not enough to prove a medical provider (e.g. doctor, surgeon, anesthesiologist, nurse, therapist, chiropractor...) breached the standard of care owed to you. We must also prove that it was the medical provider's breach that caused your injury. For example, many potential clients rightly inform us that a doctor failed to diagnose an ailment—often cancer. In these situations, even though the doctor may have been negligent, we must establish that "but for" the doctor's negligence, the injury would not have been as severe, or in the worst of scenarios, that a death could have been prevented.

South Carolina law refers to this crucial element of a medical malpractice case as "causation." Therefore, we must prove not only the medical provider's negligence, but also show that it was the provider's negligence that caused the injury or death.

2. I have yet to see a South Carolina doctor willing to pay off a patient rather than submit a medical malpractice claim to his/her insurance company

South Carolina doctors are required to possess malpractice insurance. Doctors' malpractice policies protect them against personal liability. Thus, when a malpractice claim is filed, it is the insurance company, not the doctor, who is responsible for any payout. It is also the insurance company that pays to defend the lawsuit on the doctor's behalf. For these reasons, doctors rarely—if ever—pay off patients to avoid a medical malpractice action. If you have been injured by an act of medical malpractice in South Carolina, I encourage you to contact me immediately rather than attempting to settle the claim for a minimal sum with the care provider.

3. Medical Malpractice cases are expensive, but litigation costs may be advanced by a South Carolina injury lawyer

When I represent the victim of medical malpractice, I advance costs associated with the lawsuit. These costs include the fee for a medical expert. In South Carolina, a medical expert is required to provide an affidavit in support of the lawsuit. Economists and lifecare planners may also be called upon to calculate the lost earnings and medical expenses the injured party suffered due to the act of medical malpractice.

4. If a governmental entity or medical professional working for a governmental entity caused your injury, you may have only two (2) years from the time you were harmed to file suit

Government hospitals and its employees are protected by a two (2) year statute of limitations in South Carolina. There are, however, times when rather than having only two years from the date of injury to file suit, you may have two years from the time you discovered or should have discovered the injury. Non-governmental defendants are generally protected by a three (3) year statute of limitations. The law is slightly different for minors, but in no event can suit be brought more than six (6) years after the date of injury. Due to the potentially harsh consequences the statute of limitations can produce, I encourage you to contact my office as soon as you suspect that you or a loved one has suffered from an act of medical malpractice.

5. Before bringing a medical malpractice lawsuit, we may have to file a number of other documents as required by South Carolina law

The South Carolina legislature has made it difficult for ordinary citizens injured by medical providers to recover damages. This is an unfortunate reality of "tort reform" laws written by special interest groups and insurance lobbyists. At present, we must secure an expert affidavit prior to ever filing a lawsuit. Along with the expert affidavit, we are required to submit a "Notice of Intent" to file suit, a short and plain statement of the facts substantiating your medical malpractice claim, and answers to interrogatories—all before we are even allowed to file suit. Furthermore, we must engage in mediation with defendants and their attorneys prior to initiating litigation. Put simply, victims of medical malpractice face a high, expensive hurdle to South Carolina's courtrooms. It may therefore be in your best interest to have an attorney on your side when pursuing damages against medical providers. As a SC injury lawyer, I take pride in representing medical malpractice victims during their time of need, and would be honored to speak with you.

THREE THINGS YOU SHOULD KNOW ABOUT NURSING HOME ABUSE AND NEGLECT IN SOUTH CAROLINA

First, bed sores (i.e. pressure sores) are one of the most common forms of nursing home injury in the nation. Bed sores can develop into life-threatening, decubitus ulcers if not properly treated. This problem is highlighted by the fact that as of 2001, decubitus ulcers formed the basis for nearly 50% of all nursing home litigation.

Second, the average award in nursing home negligence cases was $406,000 a decade ago. Punitive damages were awarded in nearly 20% of these cases. Along with bed sores, nursing home patients are susceptible to hip fractures, dehydration, malnutrition, prescription medication errors, and abuse. Many of these injuries and ailments would not occur but for the negligence of nursing home employees. I believe that as a society we have a responsibility to care for our seniors, to honor their sacrifices, and to protect them when they are most vulnerable. South Carolina law states that nursing homes must fulfill a number of duties to its patients. When nursing homes fail to meet their duties, causing harm to the elderly, they must be held accountable. To do otherwise would endanger the safety of every nursing home resident in our state.

Third, despite photographic evidence, immense suffering on the part of the patient, and in some cases death, insurance companies vigorously defend nursing home cases. For instance, defense experts may argue that decubitus ulcers are instead caused by diabetes. Defense attorneys might also assert that a decubitus ulcer was clinically unavoidable. Fortunately, a patient's medical records, including: intake forms, nurses' notes, lab reports, and discharge summaries will often provide evidence as to whether an individual was properly treated. In those cases where the nursing home failed to properly care for a patient, thus resulting in harm, juries have shown little mercy.

Should you have questions, or if you would like to discuss a nursing home case with a Columbia, South Carolina personal injury lawyer, I would be honored to speak with you.[1]

---

1 Stevenson, David and Studdert, David. "The Rise of Nursing Home Litigation: Findings from a National Survey of Attorneys," Health Affairs, 22,

3 THINGS YOU SHOULD KNOW ABOUT ATV SAFETY

ATVs are fun. They go fast, take you places a car never could, and are enjoyed by 1000s of families and children across the country. While ATVs also present risks, many dangers can be avoided by following a few safety rules. As a child, I watched friends violate these safety rules and barely escape life-changing accidents. I am familiar with the heartbreak and devastation that occurs when other riders are not so fortunate. I therefore offer the following safety tips, drawn from the ATV Safety Institute, in hopes that together we can build a safer, healthier community:

1. **Never operate an ATV on a public roadway.** ATVs are designed for off-road use only. Pavement may seriously affect handling and control. Driving an ATV on a public road or highway is also dangerous because other motorists may fail to see you.

2. **Always wear a helmet and dress for riding.** ATVs are not for "Sunday drives." They are meant to be taken in the woods. However, riding off-road requires long sleeves, pants, boots, and gloves. Riders should also wear goggles to avoid damage caused by debris, thorns, and other hazards.

3. **Supervise riders under the age of 16.** Your supervision will ensure that everyone is riding an

no. 2 (2003): 219-229.

age-appropriate ATV, and that children are riding at safe speeds. Riding with your children can also guarantee that multiple people are not hopping on single-rider ATVs.

South Carolina accident attorneys have been instrumental in getting legislation – most notably Chandler's Law – passed that will protect ATV riders. Nonetheless, laws are not always followed. Nor are they always as persuasive as the positive example and supervision parents can provide. Please visit the ATV Safety Institute's website (atvsafety.org) or call me should you have any questions regarding South Carolina ATV law or accident prevention. I would be honored to speak with you.

PREMISES LIABILITY: WHAT IT MEANS AND WHY IT MATTERS

I have represented a number of people in claims and lawsuits arising out of injuries sustained due to unsafe property conditions. These claims and lawsuits are known as premises liability actions. "Premises" simply means property. "Liability" is a legal term for responsibility. So a "premises liability" action is one that alleges another party is responsible for an injury you suffered while on their property. Individuals, corporations, and even the government may be sued because of unsafe property conditions.

Whether a defendant will be found liable for your injury depends in part on your reason for being on the defendant's property. South Carolina law draws distinctions between what are known as invitees, licensees, and trespassers. An invitee is a person whose presence on the property in some way benefits the defendant. For example, when you eat at a restaurant, your presence on the property benefits the restaurant in that you are spending money. The restaurant is profiting from you being on its property. The law states that because these defendants benefit from your presence they owe you the highest duty of care. Specifically, they must take safety precautions to eliminate or warn of unreasonable risks. While defendants will often claim they were unaware of the dangerous condition, actual knowledge is not required to win a premises liability case. So long as the danger existed long enough that it could have been discovered and fixed prior to the invitee's accident, a defendant may still be found liable.

Licensees are different than invitees, and are not given the same protections under South Carolina law. You can think of licensees as people who are on another's property with permission, but who provide no financial benefit to the property owner. Rather, licensees are on the premises primarily for their own benefit. For instance, when you are having dinner at someone else's home, the law considers you an invitee. Your friend is allowing you into his home to have dinner, but is not profiting financially. Your primary purpose in being on the premises is to enjoy your friend's company and have a (free) dinner. Property owners are not liable to licensees unless the owner's own activities or some hidden danger results in harm to the licensee. A faulty step or rail are examples of hidden dangers.

An impromptu fireworks show put on by the homeowner or his son is an example of activity that, if it resulted in harm to a visitor, could result in liability for the property owner.

Trespassers are owed no duty by the landowner. If someone trespasses onto your property and suffers injury, you will not be found at-fault except in the rarest of cases. However, you cannot set traps for trespassers. The classic example of the spring gun at the barn door could land the barn owner in prison, and leave his insurance company or family fighting a wrongful death lawsuit.

In sum, premises liability addresses the responsibilities of property owners to their patrons, social guests, trespassers, and every other type of visitor under the sun, all of whom will be classified as either invitees, licensees, or trespassers. This area of law is nuanced. Cases are fact specific. It is not as simple as slip and falls and stereotypes pushed on the public by insurance giants. And though I have written about owners in this article, note that the same laws of premises liability generally apply to lessees, tenants, and any other party in possession or control of the property where an accident occurs.

PRODUCTS LIABILITY: A FANCY WAY OF SAYING SOME THING IS UNSAFE

Products liability is taught in law school and discussed at legal seminars. Even though I am a South Carolina injury lawyer, I have never liked the term "products liability," and certainly do not use it more than necessary when speaking with clients.

While the law surrounding products liability is quite complex, the term can be made simple. It is really just a fancy way of saying some "thing" is unreasonably dangerous. For instance, if the blade on a power saw comes unhinged and injures you even though you were following instructions, the power saw is clearly unsafe. Likewise, when Toyota gas pedals were getting stuck and preventing drivers from stopping, the cars posed great danger.

In South Carolina, we must prove one of three things to establish a "products liability" claim. They are as follows:

1. Manufacturing defect;

2. Design defect; or

3. Defective warning.

Manufacturing defects occur when a product does not turn out the way it was intended. These problems might develop while a product is on the assembly line. Consider the power saw example above. The blade may have come off because someone on the assembly line forgot to tighten a screw or fasten a bolt. This act of negligence created a manufacturing defect, which in turn resulted in an unsafe product. The manufacturer would therefore be liable for any injury to you caused by the dangerous saw. This is what "products liability" is all about – holding the party who gave you the unreasonably dangerous product responsible for your injury.

Design defects happen when a product is manufactured exactly as planned, but the design itself is flawed. You may have seen the movies or remember the cases about exploding cars. These cases involved design defects, where gas tanks could blow up if a car was struck a certain way. Similarly, there are current suits involving medical products, such as artificial hips, where it has been alleged that the products have design defects. In sum, if a product is unreasonably dangerous because its design is inherently flawed, any injury caused by the product may be grounds for suit.

Defective warnings can also provide the basis for a products liability suit. Do you remember the last time you or a family member bought a lawnmower? All lawnmowers come with warnings. Some warnings are obvious: "Keep Hands & Feet Away From Moving Blade;" "Always Make Sure Lawnmower is Turned Off Before Cleaning Chute." However, what if the lawnmower you purchased presented dangers that were not so obvious? In these situations, the manufacturer and seller must provide you with adequate warnings. When they fail do to so, they could be liable.

I can assure you that products liability is one of the most nuanced and challenging fields of law. Nonetheless, at its core, it is all about whether some "thing" is unreasonably dangerous. When an unsafe product causes injury, the manufacturer, seller, and everyone in the supply chain might be responsible for your harm.

DOG BITES: SOUTH CAROLINA & CALIFORNIA HAVE SOMETHING IN COMMON

I own an English Bulldog named Rex that I love like a son. And like any good father, I will discipline Rex. I will teach him right from wrong, and that actions have consequences. Rex will also be rewarded for good behavior, loved and nurtured. However, the law in South Carolina basically holds that no matter how much training, supervision, and care I show my dog, if he ever injures someone, I am liable. *That's right, even a Columbia, South Carolina personal injury lawyer can get sued.*

Our courts follow what is known as the "California Rule." The state legislature has likewise adopted a law that essentially states a dog's owner is strictly liable for any injury caused by their pet. While our judges have worked hard to prove "strict liability" is not the law in South Carolina when it comes to dog bites, as a dog owner I consider myself strictly liable for any harm Rex causes. In other words, I do not have to be negligent to be responsible.

I could be walking my English Bulldog out of Petco, where he had just received some type of doggy diploma, when he snaps at a pedestrian, causing her to fall off the sidewalk. If the innocent pedestrian falls and breaks her wrist, I would unfortunately be liable for her injury even though I had Rex on a leash with his diploma in my hand. This example – *not my best* – hopefully illustrates the difference between strict liability and negligence. In this case, I did not do anything wrong, but I would nonetheless be responsible for my dog's act and the harm it caused.

Similarly, if Rex ever bites a non-trespasser without provocation, I am liable - even if it is the first time he has shown aggression. The law may seem harsh, but it was never intended to punish dog owners. Rather, the law's intent is to protect our communities, and to ensure that the financial burden of an accident does not fall solely on the shoulders of an innocent victim. South Carolina law is certainly not perfect, but as a dog owner and injury attorney I accept my responsibilities, and will do everything in my power to guarantee that no person is ever harmed by my dear Rex.

WRONGFUL DEATH: GUIDANCE FOR FAMILIES WHO HAVE LOST A LOVED ONE

In this world, there are no words or acts that can bring back someone we love. When another person or business' negligence causes a loved one's death, the hurt and confusion can be devastating. The sudden loss of a family member often leaves survivors with far more questions than answers.

Though many of the answers are beyond my or any person's understanding, I am committed to guiding families through the legal maze that is created when another's negligence or recklessness ends the life of a loved one. Fatal accidents often give rise to wrongful death claims, which are designed to compensate grieving families, and hold negligent parties accountable for their actions.

In my time as a wrongful death attorney, I have listened to families describe the devastating impact that a sudden loss had on them. I have heard stories of fatal auto accidents, nursing home abuse, and seemingly healthy people who never left the hospital. Their stories are heart-wrenching, their need for justice undeniable. It is their stories—their call for justice—that motivate me to battle insurance companies over the rights of grieving families.

Since we cannot reverse time and undo harm, we are required to measure justice by jury awards and settlements. It is an imperfect means, but is often a family's only way to recover the financial and emotional loss they suffer when another's negligence robs them of a loved one.

My job is to guide families through the process, to protect their rights, and to secure compensation.

May all those we have lost rest in peace, and may their memory be forever blessed.

CHAPTER 4

Workers' Compensation

5 THINGS YOU SHOULD KNOW ABOUT SC WORKERS' COMPENSATION LAW

1. **South Carolina Workers' Compensation is a "no-fault" system**

SC Workers' Compensation Commissioners (i.e. Judges) do not weigh negligence or assess fault in determining whether you are entitled to compensation for your on-the-job injury. Though compensation may be barred due to intoxication, horseplay, fraud and other defenses, your negligence will not prevent you from recovering damages if you were injured at work. In addition, your employer's negligence will not increase the value of your case. South Carolina's workers' compensation laws simply state that you are entitled to losses that result from your work-related injury. Unless you intentionally hurt yourself, were injured due to your own intoxication, or engaged in fraud, you are likely entitled to compensation. A South

Carolina workers' compensation attorney can help you pursue the benefits our law promises.

2. Your employer cannot fire you in retaliation for filing a workers' compensation claim without making himself/herself liable to you in civil court

South Carolina law prohibits employers from engaging in retaliatory firings. If you are fired in retaliation for filing a workers' compensation claim, you can directly sue your employer in civil court. While my firm does not handle suits of this nature (i.e. wrongful/retaliatory termination), our workers' compensation experience has allowed us to develop relationships with a number of employment law attorneys. We would be pleased to refer you to one of these attorneys should you be the victim of an unjust, retaliatory firing.

3. Your employer's workers' compensation insurance carrier or fund, not your boss, is responsible for compensating you for your work injury

Many South Carolinians are reluctant to seek compensation for their work injuries because they are afraid it will cost their employer thousands of dollars. The truth, however, is that your employer's insurance company—not your boss—is generally the party responsible for drafting checks and ensuring medical care is provided. Though your claim may result in a premium increase for your employer, this cost is often minimal to the loss you bear should you fail to file a claim.

4. SC Workers' Compensation laws are designed to pay for your medical care, the time you miss from work, and your permanent degree of injury

After suffering an on-the-job injury, you should immediately notify your supervisor/employer. If you think medical treatment is necessary, you should ask to be sent to the doctor. From that point forward, your employer's workers' compensation carrier (i.e. insurance company) is responsible for all medical care that "tends to lessen your degree of disability"; in other words, medical care that will improve your condition. The key is that only treatment authorized by the carrier will be paid for—except in the case of emergency, where the carrier could not be contacted or reached. We will work with the insurance company to ensure that you receive necessary treatment in a prompt fashion, though this process can be frustrating for clients and attorneys. Put simply, getting the insurance company to approve medical care, even when recommended by the treating physician, is not always easy.

If a doctor places you out of work, or your employer cannot accommodate your restrictions, you are entitled to weekly compensation. The amount of weekly compensation equals approximately 2/3s of your average pre-tax wages/salary prior to the injury. Once you've reached what is known as "maximum medical improvement", a doctor will assign you an "impairment rating". You are entitled to additional compensation based in part on your impairment. We do caution, however, that in some instances, years pass between a client's injury and the time they reach maximum medical improvement. Furthermore, the SC Workers' Compensation Commission does not take pain or suffering into account when determining how much money you receive at the conclusion of your claim.

5.   If someone other than your boss or a co-worker caused your injury, you may be able to pursue a civil action in addition to your workers' compensation claim

I have handled cases where a client was injured at work due to the negligence, recklessness or intentional acts of a "third party". For instance, if you suffered a sudden fall at work due to a hazard created by a janitorial company, we would likely pursue two claims. The first against your employer's insurance carrier, the second against the janitorial company. Civil actions allow you to recover money damages that workers' compensation does not, among them damages for mental anguish, physical pain, and lost enjoyment of life. In other words, additional benefits designed to give you back the life you enjoyed prior to your injury may be available should your claim allow for what we call a "third party action".

WHAT DOES A SOUTH CAROLINA PERSONAL INJURY OR WORKERS' COMPENSATION ATTORNEY DO TO EARN A CONTINGENCY FEE?

Even in law school, I didn't quite understand what most lawyers do all day. I thought criminal defense attorneys spent a lot of time at jails or in trial, and that corporate attorneys were responsible for closing big deals. I also shared the belief that paralegals did most of the work while the attorney billed time.

It took one day in practice to begin understanding why many lawyers arrive to the office at 8 or 9 in the morning, and don't get home until the same time in the evening (usually with a file or two tucked under their arm). In my personal injury, workers' compensation, and civil litigation practice, I don't profit off billable hours. My firm's revenue is based on contingency fees. In other words, I receive 30-40% of any award (i.e. settlement funds or money damages) collected at the end of a case. If my client doesn't receive an award, I don't charge a penny. It is therefore critical that I select the right cases.

So what do I do to earn my fee as a personal injury and workers' compensation lawyer? First, I spend meaningful time getting to know my clients and the facts of their case. Rather than having potential clients meet with a paralegal during the initial consult, I meet with them personally. If I choose to represent the client, my firm begins collecting and organizing medical records, corresponding with the at-fault party's insurance company, and building a hard copy file. We may then take photographs and video, obtain loss wage information, and draft demand letters in an attempt to resolve the matter without having to file suit. However, if the at-fault party's insurance company refuses to settle the case for a fair sum, we proceed with litigation.

After filing suit, I might retain medical and safety experts, lifec-are planners, private investigators, technology consultants, and a host of other professionals, as effective advocacy often requires such measures.

Finally, I work hard to keep clients informed from the moment of our first meeting until their case concludes. Phone calls are returned, clients are treated with the respect and compassion they deserve, and great efforts are made to maximize the value of every case.

WHAT INFO WILL YOUR COLUMBIA, SC WORKERS' COMPENSATION LAWYER NEED WHEN YOU CALL AND WHEN YOU MEET

I receive calls from people in search of answers. Some of them worked their entire lives, only to have that ability taken from them in an instant when they were injured on the job. They do not know how they will pay bills, provide for their families, or obtain medical treatment. To answer their questions, it is essential that SC workers' compensation lawyers first gather basic information related to the accident. Therefore, when you call my office, or any SC workers' compensation attorney, please be ready to answer some of the following questions (it will only take a few minutes, but often helps your case a great deal in the long run):

1. How did the accident happen?

2. Who were you working for when it happened?

3. When did the accident happen?

4. Where did the accident happen?

5. Did you notify your employer of the accident?

6. Did your employer send you for medical treatment?

7. Who have you treated with since that time?

8. Are you still receiving medical treatment?

9. Have you missed any time from work because of the accident?

10. Are you receiving a Workers' Compensation check for the time you've missed from work?

11. How long have you been out of work?

12. Could you go back to work, or does a doctor have you out of work?

13. Have you been giving your work excuses to your employer?

14. When is your next doctor's/physical therapy appointment?

15. Were there any witnesses to your accident?

16. What hurts right now?

17. Has anyone from the Workers' Compensation insurance company contacted you?

18. What company are they with?

19. What is the best number(s) to reach you?

20. What is the best time for me to call you?

After learning these essential facts, I will often set up a free consultation with a potential client. If you come in for one of these consultations, there are a number of items I need you to bring. Once more, having these items on hand will greatly benefit your case and usually helps move the case forward a little quicker.

In addition to any incident report you may have, please bring: *all medical records, medical bills, your health insurance card, photos related to the accident//injuries, and any other documents that you would not have had it not been for the accident.* In other words, I want to see everything related to the accident, as well as your medical treatment. I do not need your complete medical file, I only need to know where you have treated since the injury, so that my office can request your records from those facilities.

SC workers' compensation attorneys should present the strongest evidence—from the incident report, to the photos, to the medical reports—when pursuing your case. Collecting this evidence begins the moment you walk into my office and will not stop until I believe we have built the best possible case given the facts of your accident. Insurance companies and the Workers' Compensation Commission are not impressed by our words, but rather the evidence we present. Help me in this pursuit by being prepared to answer the above questions, and by bringing with you the documents I have listed.

IF IT MAKES YOU BETTER, THE INSURANCE COMPANY MUST PAY FOR IT, AND OTHER TRUTHS REGARDING INJURED EMPLOYEES' MEDICAL TREATMENT

According to South Carolina law, injured employees are entitled to all medical treatment that "tends to lessen their degree of disability." In other words, your employer's insurance company must pay for all medical care that helps heal you after an on-the-job accident. Because the insurance company is paying for your treatment, they often attempt to control which doctors you see and what treatment you receive. While insurers have a right to participate in the selection of your doctors, this right is not absolute. Furthermore, treating physicians rather than insurance companies, should decide which procedures are necessary for your health. All medical treatment that an authorized treating physician declares necessary to lessen your degree of disability, must ultimately be approved and paid for by the insurance company.

Nonetheless, workers' compensation insurance carriers often disagree with doctor's findings and refuse to authorize necessary treatment. When this occurs, we file for a hearing before the SC Workers' Compensation Commission. If the insurance company continues to dispute the need for treatment, we will present the medical evidence along with your testimony at the hearing. A Workers' Compensation Commissioner will then decide whether the treatment should be approved. The process of filing for a hearing, having it placed on the docket, appearing before the Commission, and having treatment ordered, can take months. During that time, your injury might worsen. In the long run, delaying necessary medical care often increases the amount of money an insurance company will have to pay you.

When a doctor finds that additional medical treatment will do nothing to improve your condition, she will declare that you have reached "maximum medical improvement" (MMI). Reaching MMI does not mean future medical care is unneeded. Instead, it is an indication that such care cannot relieve you of permanent impairment. For example, if you fracture your arm you may never regain full strength and mobility. Even after months of medical treatment, you may experience pain at the injury site or tingling along the nerves. At some point, medical treatment might help sustain your health, but it will never make your arm 100%. That is the point at which a doctor will state you have reached MMI. When an injured worker achieves MMI, the treating physician will issue findings pertaining to impairment and the need for future treatment. If medical care beyond the date of MMI would "lessen the period of disability," the insurance company must pay for such care. In simple terms, the law requires your employer's workers' compensation carrier to pay for all treatment that makes you better and keeps you well.

I have dedicated myself to injured workers' health and recovery. Everyday my firm works to ensure our workers' compensation clients receive the treatment they need from doctors they trust. When insurance companies refuse to follow the law, SC workers' compensation attorneys must be prepared to hold them accountable, and fight to obtain needed treatment for clients.

SC WORKERS' COMPENSATION SETTLEMENTS: OPTIONS & OPPORTUNITIES

As a workers' compensation lawyer, my job is to maximize the value of an injured worker's case. Along with medical benefits and payments for time missed from work, I fight to ensure injured workers receive fair settlements/awards for any permanent harm. SC Workers' compensation cases may conclude in one of three ways:

1) A full and final release, known as a "clincher" agreement

2) A settlement agreement between the parties that may allow for further medical treatment

3) A hearing in front of a Workers' Compensation Commissioner (i.e. judge)

The first option, a "clincher" agreement, brings the case to conclusion more quickly than options two and three. By "clinchering" a claim, the employer is forever released from all future liability pertaining to the work injury. The injured worker is essentially taking responsibility for any additional treatment that may be required. Even when a claim is "clinchered," we demand that our client be compensated for all future treatment needed to maintain their condition or lessen the recovery time. For these reasons, clincher agreements often cost employers' insurance companies more money up front and result in a larger settlement figure. Put simply, employers and their insurers must pay good money for a final release from liability. Clincher agreements are appealing to many clients who want a greater sum. Clients who require no further treatment or possess health insurance are also more likely to seek a clincher agreement so they can once more choose their own doctors rather than treat with providers workers' compensation was paying.

Other clients may best be served by a settlement agreement that "keeps the medicals open for one year." This option might result in a less significant initial payment, but in turn permits the injured worker to seek additional treatment within one year if the individual experiences a "substantial change of condition." For example, if a client tore her rotator cuff at work, undergoes arthroscopic surgery, but continues to experience daily pain, muscle fatigue, and a clicking noise at the injury site, she may elect to "keep the medicals open" rather than clincher the case. By electing this option, the client can receive additional treatment for her shoulder injury within one-year of the settlement provided we can establish she experienced a "significant change of condition" since the settlement date. Additionally, all future medical care that lessens the period of disability must be paid for by the insurer. Clients who require considerable future treatment or lack health insurance often choose this option.

Finally, if the employer's insurance company refuses to offer a fair settlement amount, we will request that a SC Workers' Compensation Commissioner decide the case. When this occurs, my client and I appear before the Commission, and present the evidence. I generally have the client testify as to the facts of the injury, medical treatment, current condition, education, work history, and any other matter that may affect the ruling. I also subpoena witnesses and examine them as to their knowledge of the case when it furthers the client's interest. Once all evidence is submitted, a Workers' Compensation Commissioner will decide what, if any, award an injured worker will receive. When cases are decided by the Commission, the medicals remain open for one year. Commissioners also have authority to order future treatment that lessens the period of disability.

SC workers' compensation attorneys must understand the client's wants and needs when advising on settlement matters. Therefore, when selecting an SC workers' compensation attorney, consider that individual's experience with this highly nuanced field of law, as well as the level of attention your case will receive from the attorney.

IS WORKERS' COMPENSATION AN INJURED EMPLOYEE'S ONLY REMEDY? NOT ALWAYS

South Carolina's workers' compensation laws are designed to provide injured employees with a means of recovery that is predictable and uniform. Workers' compensation is a "no-fault"system. Employees may generally receive benefits and medical care even if they were at fault. Negligence plays no role in most workers' compensation cases. However, in some instances an employee may pursue both workers' compensation benefits and a civil action. Third party actions are permitted where an employer or co-worker intentionally harms you. Examples of "third party" civil actions also include times where someone other than your employer or co-worker caused your injury. For instance, if you were delivering goods in the course of your employment, and a driver struck your car after running a red light, we may be able to seek workers' compensation and civil claims.

In such cases, I file a workers' compensation claim with your employer's insurance company, and a civil claim with the at-fault driver's insurer. Your medical treatment and 2/3s of your lost wages will be paid through the workers' compensation claim. Additionally, workers' compensation should pay you for any permanent injury.

Unlike a workers' compensation action, you could receive settlement funds from the at-fault driver's insurer for pain, mental anguish, lost quality of life, and other non-economic damages. The auto insurance company must also pay for medical expenses and lost wages, even though you already received a portion of those benefits from the workers' compensation carrier. The law allows double recovery to ensure the at-fault party is held responsible for his negligence.

However, if proceeds are recovered from both insurance companies, the workers' compensation carrier may have a "lien" (i.e. reimbursement) on the case. My firm works with the workers' compensation carrier to reduce the lien as much as possible in order to maximize an injured party's recovery. I have handled a number of these "third party actions," then negotiated down the liens.

If you have sustained an on-the-job injury, workers' compensation benefits are available, barring some exceptions. In certain cases, you may also be entitled to recover damages from a third party due to that person's negligence or willfulness. Put simply, workers' compensation is not always an injured employee's only remedy. A personal injury action may be available to you as well.

THREE KEY BENEFITS YOUR SC WORKERS' COMPENSATION ATTORNEY SHOULD FIGHT TO OBTAIN FOR YOU

South Carolina's injured workers are entitled to three main benefits: medical treatment, payment for time missed due to injury, and compensation for any permanent disability. When a worker sustains an on-the-job injury, she should immediately notify her employer. The employer should then send the injured employee to the doctor. All medical treatment related to the injury is supposed to be paid for by the employer's insurance company. The same way we have auto insurance to protect other drivers and ourselves, most SC employers possess workers' compensation insurance to protect their employees. State law requires businesses with four or more employees to carry workers' compensation coverage. Therefore, when an injured worker seeks medical care, it is generally the insurance company, not the employer, who is paying for treatment. The insurer must pay for all treatment that "tends to lessen the degree of disability." In other words, they have to pay for all medical care that helps heal an injured worker. Even when an employee has reached "maximum medical improvement," the insurance company may still have to pay for future treatment.

If an employee is unable to work because of an on-the-job injury, or the employer cannot offer work that falls within a doctor's restrictions, the injured worker should receive what most people call a "workers' compensation check." The legal term for these payments is "temporary total disability." The amount of the check depends on how much money an employee was earning prior to the accident. Temporary total disability (TTD) payments equal two-thirds (2/3) of an employee's pretax, weekly wage. For instance, if you earned an average of $600 per week before the injury, you would receive weekly TTD payments in the amount of $400. As an SC workers' compensation lawyer, I subpoena wage information from our state's Department of Employment and Workforce to guarantee insurance companies are paying workers' compensation clients the full amount they are owed.

When an injured worker reaches MMI, the treating doctor will be asked to assign an "impairment rating." The impairment rating, along with the injured worker's education, work history, and physical restrictions are all taken into account when determining the degree of disability. For example, a torn meniscus may require arthroscopic knee surgery. Even after the surgery, the injured worker may experience swelling and daily pain. This may result in the treating physician issuing a 5% impairment rating. If the worker had only a high school education and a work-history defined by heavy labor, he may never return to his former job. Furthermore, he may be unable to find a sit-down job. For these reasons, a 5% impairment rating could translate to 15% disability. The same injury might only produce a 10% disability for lifelong administrators, because such workers are not as affected by the impairment.

If you think this sounds confusing, I do as well. However, it is my job to guide clients to the best possible outcome. My firm is committed to the rights of injured workers and the guarantees South Carolina law provides. We fight to ensure all medical treatment is provided, that clients are receiving TTD checks in a timely manner, and that insurance companies properly compensate workers for all permanent injuries and effects.

THE WHAT, WHEN AND WHY OF SC WORKERS' COMPENSATION CHECKS

If you are hurt on the job in South Carolina, your employer's insurance company will likely have to compensate you for the time you miss from work. The amount of compensation you receive is based on two-thirds (2/3) of your pre-tax, weekly earnings. For instance, if you grossed an average of $600 per week before your accident, you would be entitled to weekly payments of $400. Most people refer to these weekly payments as "workers' compensation checks." In legal terms they are known as payment for "temporary total disability." The idea is that you are temporarily unable to perform your job, and should therefore be compensated. However, many South Carolina workers struggle to get by on only two-thirds their wage.

I inform my clients of all their options. At times, one of these options includes seeking another job within the doctor's restrictions. For instance, if a heavy laborer is injured in a factory and the doctor restricts him to light duty, yet his employer has no light duty available, the client may be unable to support his family off a workers' compensation check. The client may therefore choose to apply for a new job that permits light duty work. For example, the injured worker might apply as a cashier, hotel clerk, or any other position with few physical demands. Even though the new job might only be temporary, it will allow the client to get out of the house and back on his feet.

The injured person would continue to receive a workers' compensation check unless the wages from his new job matched his pre-accident earnings. Specifically, the insurance company would have to issue weekly checks for two-thirds of the difference between his old and new earnings. This type of workers' compensation check is known in the law as payment for "temporary partial disability." Once again, the idea is that you must be compensated if you are unable to complete a full return to your former job. Temporary partial disability payments are therefore made even if you return to your former workplace at a lower salary or on a part-time basis. Like all other workers' compensation checks, you should continue to receive temporary partial disability payments until an authorized doctor determines that you have reached maximum medical improvement.

While two-thirds of your pre-accident earnings or the thought of working part-time for a new employer is frightening, it can often be the difference between paying bills and bankruptcy. South Carolina workers' compensation attorneys guide clients through these difficult times, and fight to ensure full benefits are received. It is why I am proud to call myself a workers' compensation attorney, and one of the reasons I find great satisfaction in my job.

WHY PREEXISTING CONDITIONS AFFECT SC PERSONAL INJURY AND WORKERS' COMPENSATION CASES LESS THAN YOU BELIEVE

Many people think that a preexisting condition will prevent them from recovering in a South Carolina personal injury or workers' compensation case. They are wrong. Personal injury law is intended to place a person in the position he/she enjoyed prior to the accident. Therefore, if an accident worsens an individual's health, the injured party has a right to recovery. For example, many seniors suffer from arthritis. They take supplements and engage in home exercises to prevent their symptoms from progressing. However, when our seniors get in auto accidents or become victims of nursing home neglect, their health often worsens. They may experience increased joint pain, broken bones, or bulging discs. They may not have been in perfect health before the accident, but that does not mean the elderly receive no protection from the law. In these cases, our seniors are entitled to payment for all medical expenses and other losses they would not have incurred "but for" the other party's negligence. The same truth applies to every other injured person in South Carolina who may have a preexisting condition. Remember: in South Carolina, the defendant takes you as he finds you. To do otherwise would be a great injustice to the sick, vulnerable, handicapped, and elderly.

Likewise, South Carolina's workers' compensation laws do not punish workers for their preexisting conditions. The law expressly provides that an injured worker may recover benefits if the preexisting condition was aggravated by a work-injury. Consider for instance a production line worker who suffered a knee injury while playing with his children, five years before he tore a ligament at work. So long as the man did not lie when he applied for his job, he would likely be entitled to workers' compensation benefits.

I understand that many South Carolinians fear disclosing a preexisting condition in their job applications. However, if you commit "fraud in the application" you may not be able to receive benefits for your on-the-job injury. It can be a double-edged sword, though between deceit and honesty, the choice is clear.

As a personal injury and workers' compensation attorney, I would be honored to answer any questions you may have.

CHAPTER 5

Child Injury

SC CHILD INJURY LAW & 3 WAYS TO PROTECT YOUR CHILDREN FROM A BURN INJURY

There are few tragedies in this world greater than a child burn victim. Approximately 10,000 children suffer burn injuries in our country every year. Memories of the accident, like the scars, often last a lifetime. South Carolina child injury lawyers are confronted with these tragedies on a regular basis. While it is a child injury attorney's job to advocate on behalf of the victim, I believe it is also our job to teach the public how these accidents might be avoided. Please consider the following suggestions, taken from the *Richland County Fire Department* and *National Fire Prevention Association*:

1. **Teach your children that candles can be as dangerous as they are attractive.** Each day, 35 home fires are started by candles in the U.S. Since 2005, more than 1,000 people have been injured by home fires that

began with candles. Many times these fires start when an object is placed too close to the flame.

2. **Make sure your children are supervised when they cook.** As the child of a single-father, I learned to cook when I was young. We did not always follow this safety rule, but it is a good one. Cooking equipment is the leading cause of home fires. It is also a leading cause of home fire deaths. In addition to home fires, unattended cooking can result in stovetop burns, microwave scalding, and spill burns.

3. **Demonstrate firework safety and talk about the consequences of unsafe action.** Each year, 1000s of Americans end up in emergency rooms because of firework injuries. While many of these injuries are to hands and fingers, the large majority are to other body parts, including the head, face, and eyes. Even more disturbing, almost half of all people hurt by fireworks are under age 15. Help reduce these numbers by discussing them with your kids.

I have watched families endure the hardships brought on by burn accidents. Though I receive great satisfaction fighting to ensure justice for young victims, I wish there was no such thing as childhood injury. Let us all therefore work together to make our communities, homes, and families safer.

SOUTH CAROLINA DAYCARE LAWS: YOUR CHILD HAS THE RIGHT TO FREEDOM FROM DANGEROUS CAREGIVERS

As a child injury attorney, I can assure you that your children have the right to freedom from dangerous caregivers. State law requires background checks to be performed on all daycare center staff members. These background checks are intended to guarantee that no one caring for your child has ever been convicted of certain crimes, including those against minors. Only after an interviewee's background check—including fingerprint testing—is complete, may that individual begin working at a South Carolina daycare. Unfortunately, many "child development centers" break the law and fail to complete full background investigations. When they break the law, they place the most vulnerable members of our community at risk. If your child is currently enrolled at a South Carolina daycare, ask the center's director whether fingerprint samples were taken from all staff members, and whether those samples were run not only through SLED's databank, but through the FBI's as well. That is what state law mandates.

Caregivers must meet specific requirements in addition to having a past free of dangerous crime. First, they must be at least 18. Second, caregivers must possess at least a high school diploma or GED. (*Please note: These first two requirements have narrow exceptions that would require far too much legalese to cover.*) Third, all caregivers are required to undergo orientation with the center's director. The orientation is designed to teach caregivers about their duties, as well as the policies and procedures that affect child safety. Fourth, every caregiver must participate in at least 15 hours of training each year. Records concerning annual training are to be kept on the daycare's premises. In sum, your children have the right to a well-trained, educated, care provider who will never endanger but rather nurture and help develop them as they prepare for grade school and beyond.

As an SC Child injury lawyer, I want you to know your child's rights, as well as your own. I want you to hold your child's daycare to the highest standard. I want to do everything I can not only to represent our children's interest, but to guard it.

DOG SAFETY: MAKING SURE MAN'S BEST FRIEND NEVER BECOMES A DANGER TO YOUR CHILDREN

I recently bought an English Bulldog. His name is Theodore "Rex" Berger in honor of Teddy Roosevelt, one of our most fearless presidents. The moment I purchased Rex, he became my most loyal companion. He would do anything to protect me. I feel the same sense of loyalty to him. It is therefore my responsibility to make sure my dear friend is properly trained, cared for, and looked after. Rex can never become a danger to our community. South Carolina law recognizes my responsibilities. In fact, our law holds that if Rex ever injures another person, I am liable. That is why I must nurture, discipline, and carefully watch over him. It is not enough to send Rex to a trainer, buy a few toys, feed him twice a day, and hope nothing bad happens. My dog is my responsibility.

I am all too familiar with the harm caused by untrained and unsupervised dogs. Some of the most devastating injuries can be to children. In some instances, these injuries are the result of unexpected attacks from a neighborhood or family dog. I therefore offer the following safety tips, taken from *PETCO*, for you to consider.

1 Remind your children that the dog must be respected. Dogs are not stuffed animals. They hurt when struck and teased.

2. Discipline your dog when he plays too rough with your children. The more a dog gets away with, the more he will think is acceptable. If he begins to bite your child to the point of leaving teeth marks, the next bite could draw blood.

3. Teach your children to wake the dog up by speaking to him from a distance, rather than by shaking him. Dogs sometimes bite out of self-defense when first awoken.

4. Protect your dog from children who do not follow your safety rules. A child your dog does not know, who begins to treat him differently than any of your children ever would, might make your dog feel threatened.

5. Make sure your children understand the crate is the dog's private area. When children enter the crate, your dog could feel trapped, and snap out of fear.

Each year, 4.5 million people are bitten by dogs. Children are among the highest at risk. However, following these tips, informing yourself of other preventive measures, and putting this knowledge to use, will make South Carolina a little safer for our families and neighbors.

5 SAFETY TIPS EVERY SOUTH CAROLINA PARENT SHOULD CONSIDER WHEN SELECTING & USING A CHILD'S CAR SEAT

Each year, nearly 200,000 children are injured in auto accidents. I have seen the impact these accidents have on young people and their families. Though many injuries are unavoidable, sometimes the harm can be lessened. My job as an injury lawyer is not only to advocate on behalf of child victims, but to provide the public with information that may help them avoid accidents and lessen the consequences.

I am therefore offering the following safety tips from *seatcheck.org*. Please consider this information when selecting and using your child's car seat:

1. Children should ride facing the back of the car, until they are at least 2 years old, or until they outgrow their rear-facing safety seat.

2. Never place a rear-facing safety seat in front of a passenger air bag.

3. Children who have outgrown their rear-facing safety seat can ride facing forward, but should remain in a seat, with a harness, up to the highest weight or height allowed by the seat.

4. All children whose weight or height is above the forward-facing limit for the safety seat should use a belt-positioning booster seat until the vehicle's seat belts fit properly.

5. Always read the instructions that come with the child safety seat, then get your seat checked to make sure everything works properly.

My staff and I recognize that every case gives us the opportunity to make our community safer by holding people and companies that have violated safety rules accountable for their wrongdoing. I believe that we can also make our community safer and healthier by providing as much free legal and safety information as possible to you.

As a SC child injury lawyer, I would be honored to answer any questions you may have regarding safety regulations, negligence, and what we can do together to make our state safer for our children.

SOUTH CAROLINA DAYCARE LAWS: YOUR CHILD HAS THE RIGHT TO A SAFE DAYCARE

I can assure you that your children have the right to a safe daycare. State law regulates everything from how a daycare is to be ventilated to what type of materials must be located under playground equipment. You should never have to worry that your child will get overheated while in the care of a "child development center." Likewise, if all daycares followed the law, no parent would need to feel concern over whether the swings and slides were properly maintained. Unfortunately, not every child care center plays by the rules. While some of South Carolina's daycares are the envy of the nation, others expose our children to needless danger.

Lawmakers have attempted to promote daycare safety through a number of regulations, including:

1. Safety barriers shall be placed around all heating sources, such as radiators and hot water heaters;

2. Lighters, projectile toys, and microwave ovens shall not be accessible to children;

3. Items that may cause choking or suffocation shall be inaccessible to children for whom they are not age appropriate;

4. Electrical outlets shall be securely covered when not in use; and

5. Each deck that has over an 18-inch drop shall have a well-secured railing.

Despite regulations, safety manuals, and the fact that keeping kids safe is simply the right thing to do, many South Carolina daycare centers fall short. When these groups needlessly cause injury to our young people, I stand ready to help. As an SC child injury attorney, my job is to listen with compassion, answer questions, guide families through the legal process, and fight for justice when daycare centers and their insurance companies refuse to take responsibility.

THREE THINGS YOU SHOULD KNOW ABOUT TOY SAFETY IN SOUTH CAROLINA

First, check labels to find out where the toy was made. As you know, some countries' safety regulations are much stricter than others. Where a toy was manufactured can make the difference in what type of paint, chemicals, and other materials went into its' production.

Second, ask the store clerk about recalls, returns, and complaints. If the toy's manufacturer deals with frequent recalls, or if the toy you have chosen is often returned, you will want to know why. You can also research the toy and its manufacturer prior to making your purchase. Spending a little time conducting research and asking these questions gives you an idea whether the manufacturer and merchant truly stand behind the toy they are attempting to sell you.

Third, play with the toy before buying it or allowing your child to play with it. There are many dangers the eye overlooks but experience teaches. If you play with the toy, you will likely discover any hidden dangers the toy might pose.

Children are often my favorite clients, though their stories are among the saddest. I would not be a Columbia, SC child injury lawyer if bad things did not happen to our most vulnerable. However, there are many steps you can take to reduce the number of child injuries in South Carolina. I hope this information provides a reminder as to a few of those steps.

WHY SOUTH CAROLINA TEEN DRIVERS CRASH & HOW PARENTS CAN HELP PREVENT THESE ACCIDENTS

Auto accidents remain the number one cause of teen deaths in the United States. While a number of these accidents result from drunk driving or texting, many more are caused by passenger distraction, driver inexperience, and aggressive use. I am all too familiar with the consequences of teenage driving accidents. These accidents destroy lives, families, and friendships. I therefore offer the following safety tips, taken from *teendriversource. org*, to parents of teenage drivers:

1. Make sure your teen receives at least 50 hours of supervised practice under a wide variety of weather conditions. Most teens believe that getting a license means they're experienced. However, the majority of teenage auto accidents are caused by inexperience. For example, most teen drivers lack the know-how to detect and

respond to road hazards. Help your teenager understand that getting a permit and probationary license are baby steps. Real experience is earned over time.

2. Set a rule of no teen passengers for the first six months of independent driving, and no more than one teen passenger for the second six months of driving on their own. Two or more peer passengers more than triples the risk of a fatal crash when a teen is behind the wheel. Research also finds that teen drivers with peer passengers are more likely to be distracted just before a serious crash than teens driving alone.

3 Lead by example. Even though I rebelled as a teenager, I always knew right from wrong. My dad set a great example. He did not drink and drive. Nor did he disregard red lights, throw trash bags out the window, or speed through crosswalks. While your children may tell you they do not care what you say, they certainly watch what you do.

I believe SC injury lawyers have a responsibility not only to fight for clients, but to inform the public of safety facts and tips. It is my hope that the information contained here might one day prevent an accident. Though we cannot eliminate all risk, we can work together to make our families and communities safer.

KENNETH BERGER

5205 Forest Drive

Suite 2

Columbia, SC 29206

803-790-2800

kberger@bergerlawsc.com

www.bergerlawsc.com

WA